Tell Me The Story Again

Tell Me The Story Again

ELIZABETH CUNNINGHAM

Epigraph Books
Rhinebeck, New York

Tell Me The Story Again © 2019 by Elizabeth Cunningham

Cover photo by Ruth Cunningham

Book design by Colin Rolfe

ISBN: 978-1-948796-81-1

Library of Congress Control Number: 2019909316

Epigraph Books
22 East Market Street, Suite 304
Rhinebeck, NY 12572
(845) 876-4861
EpigraphPS.com

for the Shawangunks who welcomed me home

*In this collection of poems, many voices speak from a
time perhaps just after (or long before) our time, in a real
and magical world. Through their songs, dreams, and
dialogues, a story emerges, or many stories woven into one.*

❦

VOICES

scribe
mother rain
sorrow singer
grey cat
grey mouse
courage singer
temple sweeper
sword woman
goat boy
mother goat
stone mountain/stones
ravens
ancient dreamer
the man who does not speak
merry drunk
storm singer
morose fool
great oak
stream
stillness
red oak
skeleton woman
the grannies: Onyx, Opal, Ruby, and Lapis Lazuli
bear
the children/Abelia
flying pig

scribe song

the scribe waits under the oak
watching the last leaves fall
some red, some rust, some
holding the green edge of fire

these are the leaves
these are the leaves
of the ancient book
the story is ending
tell me the story again

the scribe waits for the river
or mountain, the small brave mouse
or shadowing raven, ready
to write the translation

these are the wings
these are the feet
of the unwritten book
the story's beginning
tell me the story again

the scribe waits, scrapes
the flesh of her story
down to the bone, her own
blood will do for ink.

this is the bone
this is the blood
of the book she is writing
the story still spinning
tell me the story again

song to mother rain

mother rain, come down,
wrap us in your grey shawl
round and round and round.
touch the tender life
deep, deep underground
sweet mother rain, come down.

sorrow singer

loo loo loooo
aiyee way lo

there are no words for my song
loud I sing and soft
sorrow I sing, sometimes a trickle
of water over rock, sometimes
a flood. I want to be swept
away and find myself gone
but here I am again with only
a wordless song.

aiyee way lo
loo loo loooo

grey cat song

I am the grey cat.
now you see me
now I am jungle and stone.
I belong to no one
I will make your lap my own.
when you lie down with me
I am a soft grey sea,
purring into your bone.

grey mouse song

I am the grey mouse
seed-eater, seed-keeper.
I could save the world with my secret store.
no one but the cat knows who I am anymore.
she might want to eat me but she sees
the shadow I cast at night
when I dance by firelight.
my ears grow wide,
my nose grows long.
on tree trunk legs I'm strong.
I sway, still grey,
an elephant light as breeze.

sorrow singer's grave lament

and where shall we honor our dead
who are not ours anymore, now we
have left them, wandered from shore
to shore, followed water
to its hidden source to hide
in mists made of remorse?
oh, the wide plain in the sun, gone, gone.
oh, the labors, the loving, the feasting, done.

the dead are still our own,
the whole earth holds them,
our grave, too, our bed, our bone.
no, we have not left our dead,
there is nowhere to go but home.

courage singer

beloved comrade, if we never meet
I know you. we have both fought the enemy
until we found ourselves alone
limbs spinning in empty air.
we have been sold into captivity
and bought our freedom dear,
no longer knowing if we care.
comrade, we weep by the same rivers
and I tell you now, if you look up
and see the jeweled mating of the dragonfly,
if you note where the swallows nest
in the pock-marked cliffs, if you watch
the water flow by and by,
your courage will rise for the rest.
dear comrade, I may one day meet,
we have passed the test.

temple sweeper's song

they say the gods are gone from here,
they said the gods are ghosts,
dead as their devotees, but I remain
unsheltered from sun, from rain
in a roofless ruin where wildflowers
succor the last wild bees.
there is pollen and leaf and snow.
the gods still dance in motes of dust
I stir and sweep day after day,
believing still in the slightest chance
someone will come from far away, from long ago
to sweep me into the dance.
by firelight our shadows will leap
and the gods will reappear.

sword woman's song

wear your life lightly
like the garment it is, don't
clutch it to you tightly,
let it ride the wind.
sword woman, you say, where
is your armor, where is your shield?
beloved, my armor is to yield.
I fear no cliff edge.
I fly from tree to tree
landing softly on a limb,
death to one side, life
to the other, I love both
and fear neither, there is no strife,
no shield but flashing sword
bright in the sun. if you kill me
I love you still, the same
if I kill you.

goat boy's song

they call me motherless,
they call me wild, they call me
an angel or demon child.
some say my mother ran away,
some say she was stolen
or drowned when the river
was brown and swollen
and bodies stank and floated.
they say she won't come back
but they are wrong.
she came back as a goat.
she gives me milk, she keeps me warm.
she shows me how to dance on hardscrabble stone.
when the soldiers come
we shift into shadow.
my mother is magic no one can destroy,
my mother is magic and I am her boy.

stone mountain song

how can you hear my voice?
you come to me for silence
for wind in the pines
for water running underground
for the slow wheeling of vultures
over my bare height
for blue sky beyond shadow
in the strong hot light.

it was not always so.
loud rang the hammer and chisel
as I was taken piece by piece
to be millstone or city,
stripped of trees, a barren place
where only berries grew, you
stole those too, took them to your tables
miles and rivers below.

now I have taken back
mist and tree, moss and fern
and mystery. bears and snakes sleep
deep in hidden winter warmth
and wild cats roam. stay. I will
chide no more, small one,
forgotten, forgetting, alone.
cling to me now, I will be your home.

ancient dreamer's song

you don't need open eyes to see,
you don't need to be awake to wander.
the mountain thinks it's old
but I am older. if you see me,
and maybe you won't, don't
tread on my mossy bed, don't disturb
my fine-woven cloak, fresh flowers,
fallen leaves, don't disturb my powers,
bound and freed by dreams.

you there, lovers, I see what you can't,
how you cast dreams like nets
each over the other, never knowing
one day you will reel them back.
one day you will be small and real,
long shadows fallen into flawed flesh,
not eternally one but two for a time
with just a chance to learn to dance
until you lie down like me to dream.

song of the man who does not speak

does a frozen stream choose its silence?
when a bird is shot from the sky
what is the sound of its fall?
who hears the wind in the wake of a comet?

my tongue is not tangled,
it is hidden in a thicket
still as any animal of prey.
there is everything and nothing more to say.

I won't say what I saw
don't ask me.
I won't tell what I did.
you don't want to know.

silence is mercy and penance, one.
who among you wants to hear,
no war is ever done.

song of the merry drunk

I distill dew from the grass
rain from the leaves
birdsong from the breeze.
all berries are mine in their season,
wine for as long as it lasts.

vote with your feet, vote with your feet,
I sing with the redwing.
eat your peas, eat your peas,
is what poor will is really saying.
I sing with the songbirds, grok with the ravens.

no barstools here, pull up a rock.
tell me your troubles, whoever you are.
mine are all drowned, down the stream,
down my throat, so I sing you a song
all on one note, la la la, la la la, la la la, la.

come, sing with me. drowned sorrows
all flow to the sea, the faraway sea
where raucous seagulls sing off key.
the ground is soft and my snoring sweet.
no need to tiptoe, I'll sleep, then I'll drink.

storm singer

look! can you see it there
in the empty air,
whirling in the swirl of my palm?
you think, too small,
a storm is big! really,
there is not much difference at all.
listen! the storm is singing for you,
your rage, your grief,
your ecstasy unleashed.
the storm is singing to the earth,
the earth is singing to herself
and I am the keeper of the song.
I hold it in my hand,
I fold it into my heart.
don't fear the storms, fearful one,
there is no intent to harm,
a broken world must breathe.

morose fool's song

no one is laughing,
I was never funny.
there was no king, nor queen neither
to amuse or call to account for their sins
against the people, their sins
against owl and fish and wolf
against water and wind and honest work.
the powerful hide behind
the fools they thrust out front,
the ones they let us believe we chose.
the fools are us.
the bells on my cap don't jingle,
nor yet the bells on my toes.
I don't know how to cut a caper
or prophesy the doom already come.
do you notice? I can't even rhyme.

great oak song

hush now, small one.
I have not spoken yet, though I have grown
in silent rings three hundred years,
though I groan in wind that gives me
voice as light gives me
new limbs and earth opens to me
its depths where my roots taste truth
in rock and water.
come into the shelter of me
and lay down your despair,
come into the shelter of me
and be silent,
come into the shelter of me
and remember
you are a child among elders.
small one, you've forgotten your task
small one, you're forgiven before you ask.

ancient dreamer's question

life is short, time is long,
a thread spun out and out
and reeled back in.
you're caught,
day flower, hatchling, human.
time exists for you
because it ends.
for me time is motion,
circling, cycling
expanding, contracting.
time has a pulse,
but does it have a heart?
where is time's heart?

temple sweeper remembers

when the summer wind blows a certain way,
a few yellow leaves fly,
falling though it is not fall.
there is a sadness no different
from happiness and a happiness
holding sadness, same as the summer
wind holds those leaves in the air
as long as it can. then I remember the long-ago.
I remember something I called
love and maybe it was.
if I lean on my broom a certain way,
I will almost—but never quite—fall.
there is a yellow leaf on a broken stone,
the wind's offering to the vanished god.

grey mouse and grey cat duet

are you a ghost, grey cat?
I am this, I am that.
can you still pounce on me?
that is my secret, wait and see.
do you still want to eat me?
I am always hungry.
the people are hungry, shall I share my seeds?
is it your nature to share? you are not a pet.
I am a noble elephant, how can you forget?
lay them on the temple floor, if you can fit through the door.
I will lay them out in rounds and whorls like the sun.
don't trample them and spoil all the fun.
will they know I am their savior?
silly mouse, it's your secret to savor.

temple sweeper's dream

it is something I forget
in this time that is empty as dawn sky,
as the bowl scraped to the bone
once each day.

I am someone's daughter,
the chief's daughter, royal.
I am called to the banquet
not to eat but to meet the men
seated there on cushions
in the great tent, the feast laid out
untouched, like my hand
my father's enemies only pretend to kiss.
I walk slowly from man to man.
if I breathe wrong, if I think wrong,
war will come.

later I hear, they do not like my dress
embroidered with a sage's words,
with doves that all mean peace, peace, peace.
they think it is an insult just for them.

after the war, there is nothing left.
I can only remember the long-ago
in my dreams.

song to the ancient dreamer

your face a dry leaf,
your bone made of stone.
ancient dreamer, take me down
to what you know.

unknown, unknown
hear the wind moan
what I know cannot be known
only dreamed, only dreamed.

your hands trailing tendrils,
your feet made of moss,
ancient dreamer, lead me on
to what you know.

unknown, unknown
a knife edge to be honed,
what I know cannot be known
only dreamed, only dreamed.

your mouth a hollow,
you belly a mound,
ancient dreamer, take me in
to what you know.

unknown, unknown
all life is on loan.
what I know cannot be known
only dreamed, only dreamed.

stream song

water will always find a way
over or underground, down.
nothing can stand in its way for long.

water will always find a way
up to the sky, cloud, shroud,
rising again and again to fall.

water will plump grain and fruit,
grow trees and fish, run in your veins.
water will roll down your cheeks.

water makes the earth a jewel,
shining, water can be wounded, too,
fouled, misused, hoarded by your kind.

know this: water is an eternal verity.
what you think matters, doesn't.
what you scarcely notice, does.

temple sweeper dreaming

what I gave you when you left
or when I made you go,
a basket holding a heart-shaped stone.
like your heart, a few leaves, a feather.
you hurt someone (was it me?)
and now you must leave.
whatever you did, my anger is gone.
the basket holds my blessings. go.

the man who does not speak has a dream

in the dream, I know things
I do not want to know,
how a man can look at a woman,
her buttocks round as fruit, and think
she is his for the taking,
because she looks ripe.
worse, he thinks she wants to be taken,
he thinks she is blind as a berry,
without want or vision of her own.
he thinks the whole world his,
because it is there spread out before him.
I wake and wonder how a berry
feels and who is the one who cannot see.
I wake afraid the man is me.

how sword woman learned to fly

one day it happened, as I practiced
putting down my root, I rose instead,
each trajectory kept on going and going,
and so I flew, wind and cloud teaching me
how to be soft, how to swim the sky.

morose fool's lament

now that I am no one's fool,
I am a fool left holding the light.
my arm grows weary lifting
the lantern. no one looks
for me, and I search everywhere
for what I don't know, only
it is always beyond light's reach.
behind me darkness rises,
the night crabs glow at my feet,
scrabbling for truth or my toes,
it is all one to me. I walk on
into the trackless hills and wood,
more constant than the moon.

courage singer and sorrow singer duet

sometimes courage comes from the ground.
hush, my children are buried there.
from noticing one plant, different from another.
there is no comfort but the wild blue air.
or a bloom you never saw before.
beauty hurts, why would you wish for more?
a tree bends down to drop fruit in your hand.
my children starved in a barren land.
yes, I remember the salted earth, the poisoned well.
the sickened ones who walked with a bell.
we who remain must mourn and yet—
no more of courage, we owe sorrow a debt.
though the sun is cold, look, a new leaf.
I see the mold, the death beetle, the grief.
there! the grey mouse takes a seed from a stalk.
mice fouled the grain that could have been bread.
ah, sorrow singer, I will sing with you for our dead.
yes, sing with me, friend, no more talk.
sing and walk our rocky common ground.
yes, sometimes courage comes from there.
grey mouse knows the ground, one seed, then another

stillness speaks

there is a place under your breastbone
where I dwell, not the hardworking heart,
a silent pool you can't see
made of memory of water and sky.
a leaf falls there, rides the reflection
of the moon, then softens, sinks,
into the depths of me.

when you pause, one foot not quite
fallen on a mountain path,
remember me there
in the depths of you.

merry drunk and storm singer duet

why does the earth pitch like a ship?
yo ho, yo ho, the stormy sea and me,
the captain of a sinking fate.

you're drunk, you're drunk!
the night is calm, the storm
is sleeping in the mountain's lea.

why do the stars whirl me
down night's drain? my head
aches, give me a drink of rain.

you're drunk, you're drunk!
the stars are clear and almost still.
choose one and follow it over the hill.

why do you sing so sweetly?
where is your blast and roar,
your bone-drenching, icy downpour?

you're drunk, you're drunk!
pipe down! even storms must rest.
pass out on the curve of my breast.

before I sleep let's sing
a merry tune in harmony, in time
to the wavering wafer of moon.

you're drunk, you're drunk!
pass me the wine, red as the dawn,
and I'll sing you a sailor's warning.

mother rain song

I have so many children,
baby bird mouths calling,
flowers and fruit, farmers
scratching in the dust,
slowing rivers, rocks rising.

I am not the torrent,
I am not the flood, I am
milk from a cloudy breast,
falling softly, softening
everything I touch.

I wish I could be everywhere
at once. sometimes I am spread
too thin, sometimes my tears are all spent,
sometimes I too am thirsty. sing for me
the way you once did, children, dance!

I remember the sound
of feet slapping the ground, hands
clapping, fingers snapping, I remember
the voices rising when there was no dew,
plumping my clouds with longing.

sweet mother rain, you sang,
sweet mother rain, come down,
you sing, until I ache and my rain
lets down like milk, my moist breath
a benediction over the bone-dry earth.

sorrow singer's respite

when I cast my sorrow down,
I see shattered pieces on the rocks
catching light, jewel-like, sea glass,
some shards smooth, some jagged.
I hear laughter, foolish, high,
a seagull's cry. it is my voice, my voice.
what's happened to my song?

did I dash my sorrow on these rocks?
is there something succulent inside?
I only know I am rising into the air
willy-nilly against my will.
I don't know how to get back down.
where is my gravity?

you have done your worst, life,
here is my life,
this strange pattern glittering below.
you have done your worst, life,
here are our lives—and deaths
and desperations,
our craven and courageous acts,
our loves lost and tossed to the wind
to fall again, here, there,
beautiful, scattered, here, there
beautiful, gathered.

I touch ground again..
I take up my burden, it is light.
I sing my sorrow, it is sweet.

the man who does not speak
watches the ancient dreamer sleep

her hands move like sea fronds,
slowly up and down on some current
I cannot see. where has she gone?
where does she go? can I go, too,
beyond, between, to a place
where memory doesn't matter anymore?
her words are slipping down a stream,
yellow leaves, fallen, forgotten, their
green life only a dream.

the ancient dreamer hears
sorrow singer's song and remembers

what does it matter to a mother?
hero, martyr, villain, victim,
they called him.
he was my son, he was mine.
I was young and he was younger.
they cut him down before his time.
time took me far from him and farther, his
falling body, there in the distance, that shadow,
here in my heartbeat forever, that horror.
him underground and me under leaves,
years and years of fallen leaves.

merry drunk watches the temple sweeper

I am an indiscretion, a loud fart, a failed
prince long since kissed to a toad.

she is the shape of the wind
the fire's fall and leap.

the broom bends to her sweep,
the dust whirls into wings.

I'll take another swig and dance a jig.
the stars fall down laughing at my feet.

sword woman wanders

once I lived in a world of gentle
fields and rambling houses,
place after place to eat and shop.
I sparred with a lazy breeze.
that world didn't last,
it couldn't last. don't ask
me about the inbetween.
come with me to this new,
old land where the mountains
grin with jagged teeth and bears
hold sway in dark forests, a fallen fortress
teeters on a rock. creatures of prey
live where they can, eat when
they may, and I wander the ridges
and rivers, my sword free for beggars,
the lost and defrocked. it's all
real, what we thought imagined,
prophetic ravens, lairs of dragons,
schemers, dreamers, enchanters,
enchantment and the kindliness
of a stranger's fire, a neighbor's bread.
only the innocent or wise know foe
from friend. befriend the one, defend
the other, be blessed by gods and birds.

morose fool's complaint

I am a hermit now, a failed fool,
without kindness for my kind.
but he watches me, the boy,
trails after me as if I am dropping
dry crumbs and he's a hopping bird.

sometimes the goat comes, too,
sometimes not. where are his
people? there are no people,
or very few. I am one, I suppose
it's true, but not his, not his.

all right it's rainy, this shelter
will do for two. come dry yourself, boy.
do you know how to speak?
no matter, I have nothing to say.
be quiet then, listen to the rain.

mother goat watches

he claims he is a fool,
but he is canny enough to find
eggs in cliff nests, to know
where the water springs pure.
he knows how to gather nuts and berries
in season make them into winter food.
my boy can learn at his school.

temple sweeper wonders

can any task lead to god?
picking fleas off a cat,
sweeping up the mouse droppings
once again, doing whatever you must do
even if you are afraid,
even if you recoil?
doing it till the fear and revulsion
go away or you can't feel them anymore.
the sun keeps rising and setting,
the stars keep wheeling,
the moon disappears and appears.
beauty is relentless,
even if it doesn't feed you
or keep you warm.
one moment I think,
good, I've almost made it through.
the next, oh no! it's almost gone.
I sweep the floor again.
I wonder what else I am supposed to do.
god come find me, god become me,
a seeker with a broom.

sorrow singer stands still

standing still in time, its wreckage
rushing past me, this temple,
that crusade, these bones, these bombs
exploded, this gun rusted, this crib broken,
that three-legged kitchen table, this ruined painting,
this scattered farmstead, rushing, rushing.
I am a willow, bending and rooted,
I am lost to time, I am lost to myself.

song of the stones

why do you say 'heart of stone?'
what do you know of either?

we could teach you lessons
of catastrophe, the violent heave,
the deafening tumble, then
the silence, the silence,
endurance, the slow sweetness
and sorrow of water shifting
our shape, finding our faces.

here is what we ask of you,
walk among us, stand,
sit still. look till you see
our faces, till you know our faces,
learn them by heart, turn
your hearts to stone.

ancient dreamer turns her eyes to the beyond

who knows what your eyes see now,
drifting toward your crown,
lids, leaves falling slowly down
restward, rootward.
your mouth moves, no words,
an almost smile, a sigh again
too small to hear, then back to sleep,
dreams that have carried you
this far, this long.

raven talk

our talk is not idle, not
human, not sound to silence silence
but sound to make silence ring
to wring the blue from the sky
and bring it drenching down
to the bone.

storm singer

I am the fever's sweat
on the brow of the world.
I may kill you or heal you
break you or break.
maybe it had to come to this,
what must die must die,
what will live, will live.

ancient dreamer's long last dreaming

bone and breath,
a little skin stretched thin,
wounds that won't heal.
mouth a dark cavern,
a few brown teeth.
I can see the skeleton
you will be, I can see
the woman you were,
the power and beauty almost
finished, undiminished.

courage singer praises home

surely I need shelter, roof or rock or root
like any creature, and like any creature,
my home beyond home is here, under this sky.
it doesn't matter if it is grey or bright,
dark or light. I am held in this curve.
I stand on this ground under its sweep.
here my courage rises, round earth to horizon.

the scribe follows the man who cannot speak

he tells his story to the stones,
each footfall, each foot held suspended
in some remembered moment
of danger that is never done.

the scribe follows, gathering his crumbs,
flinging them into the wind
for the birds to catch on the wing.
the story is not yet begun.

which canyon will he choose,
which cave will enclose him,
which river will tempt him,
with its lethal torrent?

the scribe follows. these questions
are her own. who is she to stalk
a story he doesn't want to tell?
her task to him is abhorrent, her intention,
grace.

scribe and red oak

I see you dancing into the sun,
arms flung wide, your bark
full of eyes and smiles.

I see your feet tasting dirt,
your skin weathering in the wind.
lines and creases textured, deep.

if we look long enough
you'll look like me, *I'll look like you*
human, *tree*, becoming kin.

skeleton woman's song

I spent so long in life
learning to balance these bones,
one atop the other just so
from crown to toe.

now they stand on their own,
now they rise with the sun.
who knows what is next,
one step, another?

if my bones remember
standing, why not dance?
I am holding out my hand,
come, take a turn with me.

song to the ancient dreamer

ancient dreamer, you are the boat
and the oars and the sail,
you are the wide, slow river, too.
let me ride awhile with you,
let me remember your dreams.

ancient dreamer, catch the current,
follow the tide to the wild wide sea,
the plains of your face a shore
where I wait and keep watch,
awash on the shoals of your breath.

ancient dreamer, there is a rim
where the sky and the ocean meet
and the moon and the sun disappear.
if I don't see you when you go,
I will dream of you when I sleep.

the scribe's task

when rivers carry mountains to the strand,
she must stand midstream to catch the muddy
gold in her hand, and when she sees the sea rise
to meet the land, she must remember,
every story holds the power to surprise.

skeleton woman's winter song

no shivering flesh, joints flung free of sinew,
I am light as leaves scudding over snow,
cold as icicles darting down cliffs,
hollow as a howling chimney.
I am next of kin to mountain stone,
shimmering, shape-shifting shards of moon.
the glittering night ignites my bones.

skeleton woman greets the morning

skeleton woman sits on her haunches
in the morning sun, drinks light like coffee.
smoky mist curls in and out
of the holes that were her mouth and nose.
no one can rival her sophistication.
she is elegant to the bone.

song of the stones on the long night

we are awake, sentient, sentinel. the clouds
cloak us, ice and snow shift our shapes, the moon
passes over silently, shining and shadowing,
the stars watch with us, wheel with us.
through the long night, darkly, we give back their light.

ancient dreamer awakes

I dreamed I was a tall tree,
mightier than most.
I gave shelter to many.
my shadow was very long,
like my almost eternal life.

now I wake to an empty sky.
when the mighty fall,
the world must shift.
what will grow, I wonder,
in all the light I've left?

the scribe lost

what if a story is no more than a snail trail,
slime sticky, glistening, then gone?

or a moment's morning shining
when the dew reveals the web?

the sun is seldom true to due east or west,
but wanders a worn path south to north

spinning out light, then spooling it in again,
yielding the sky to the night.

here I am with no set course,
following this one and that, whoever

will tell me truth or maybe lies. the bees
know better where the nectar bides,

and the sticky pollen for their bread.
I hunger for my story's hidden thread.

song of the grannies

each one of us named for a stone,
Onyx, Opal, Ruby, Lapis Lazuli, each
precious missed and missing child our own.

each night we open the pouches
we carry nestled or swinging
between ample or scrawny breasts.

pebbles and shells and fingernails,
shards of unknown bones, we'll
cast them forth on the table rock

to read our daily fates. you, sister,
will be the one to eat tonight, I know
you claim you can live on a crumb.

still the auguries say your turn to dine!
we'd all compete to give our last crust,
our corpses fit only for ravenous raptors,

but dying is against our rules as long
as lost children still call for their mothers.
eat now, Onyx, the stones have spoken.

Onyx calls for a dragon

we only got here by magic.
there is no other way
through the unseen gates,
through veils that mist and lift and fall.

there are voices here.
stones sing and rivers,
shadows paint the cliffs
with hieroglyphs.

there are others here.
I hear their voices,
footstep, heartbeat.
I glimpse the swirl of a skirt.

so why should we hunger,
cast our foolish stones?
why should we not summon
some magical help?

I Onyx will climb the white rock,
brave the rattle and gleam of bone.
(who is it that follows me?)
I Onyx will summon....

a dragon, yes, that can scour
the valley for goat and sheep
to feed our remnant band.
I Onyx will ride its winged back,

and our hearth will never be cold.
no more aching fingers coaxing a spark
from stubborn flint stone.
hush, now I will intone.

here, dragon, dragon, dragon!
feed us or eat us, make an end
to mere survival. I dare you
to exist. wait! I hear you clambering

toward me, grunting as you go.
wait, where are your wings?
too small to lift your pink corpulence?
gods! I've summoned...a pig!

skeleton woman is hungry

rattlety bang and a bippity bop
clickety clack and a cha, cha, chop.
I am a walking castanet,
only I don't walk I dance,
following you,
never quite in sight.
at the drop of a voice,
I can collapse,
a pile of picked bones,
a fright in your path.

where are you going
with that pig? I want to know!
what will you do with that pig?
sizzle and snap, crackle and crack,
smoke and steam and hissing
fat, filling the empty curve
of my bones. I eat the smell
of roasting meat, hungry

hungry, hungry, in a way
you can never know while
skin and blood hide your
beautiful, waiting bones.

Opal pursues

the children surround the pig,
ring around the rosy pig.
(or is it really a boar—
those bristles, that snout, the tusks!)
Onyx swears she saw wings,
insists it's a dragon in disguise.
ha, when pigs can fly!

it's meat is what it is,
or should be, will be,
if I have my way. wait!
it's running into the forest,
the children are running behind.
what else can I do but follow?
snuffle and snort, dig and cavort

dig? the pig is digging?
where is my basket?
Ruby, Lapis Lazuli, come!
truffles for supper tonight.
the bacon can wait. wait,
what is that rising from
the fat pork back? wings? wings!

the morose fool offers his services

you, old ones, come lately, autumn rain
after a long parched summer.

you, with your following swarm
and fierce intent to feed.

I have been grumbling to the stones.
I who failed to topple the mighty,

who crushed us all. do you intend
some kind of rule? then maybe you will

need an erstwhile fool, shabby
and defeated as I am. at least

take this boy who follows me,
and the goat who follows him.

temple sweeper dreams

last night I dream the ground shakes
gently, gently.
last night I dream the trees sway,
grey trunk after grey trunk.
last night I dream the bell rings,
one peel for each step.

I am riding my elephant,
the trees are talking,
and the wide ears, breeze-blown,
hear.

temple sweeper at dawn

the sun has fallen to the bare earth floor.
some god has visited in the night.
look! seeds wind out from the center,
tiny brown, larger red and golden,
whirling out into whorls.
I dare not sweep away this promise
that must be planted,
this brightness that must be buried.

who will help me?
alone, alone, living on rain and light,
tough as a weed.
what do the gods demand of me?
who is this miracle for?

the grannies bathe in a mountain pool

there is no shame in this flesh,
in this place of rocks,
bare or lichened, smooth or creased,
just like us.
and the water flowing over rock,
relentlessly, going down,
slow or fast,
just like us.

merry drunk face down

I would like to say I wash my face with dew
like some damsel in a bawdy song
of merriment and May.

truth to tell I fell
on my face instead of my arse
and woke to see the sun rise

in a shining globe of dew.
and just beyond, what do I see?
I dare not move. the most

beautiful feet, brown and bangled,
planted just beyond my bulbous nose.
shall I close my eyes

and disappear? too late—the belled
feet tiptoe towards me,
the veiled face is bending over me.

arse first, I hoist myself aloft.
she steadies me with her steadiness.
she speaks words I don't know,

translated by her hennaed hands.
come with me, come with me!
I follow, hers to command.

the man who does not speak
mourns the ancient dreamer

she is the dusty path,
she is the shard of moon,
just out of my reach.

she has sloughed
the skin that still chafes me.
she is the disappearing flicker

of a snake's tail. there is nowhere
far enough to go. there is no
dreamlessness deep enough.

how has her silence
begotten children's voices?
laughing or crying, the same torture

to me. how can I bear this sound
without her? ancient dreamer,
take me, wake me, too.

the grannies name the children

some of them do not know their own names.
did they ever have them?
surely their mothers whispered their names
at the breast, or their fathers, proudly
lifting their children on their shoulders?
before they were lost or taken,
the mothers, the fathers,
before they were killed or worse.

we watch to see what they love,
what loves them back.
Abelia, the dark girl just tall enough to breathe
the blossoms' scent.
Berry, the boy who crawls through the blueberry barren,
fist to mouth, heedless of bears.
Sun Patch, the girl curling cat-like on the warm stone.
Spider Web, the girl who points to them
and will not let us tear or tread.
Splash the boy who leaps again and again
from high rock to deep pool.
and now a new arrival, the boy
who calls a goat his mother
son of a goat, Goat Boy.

Opal frets

summer warms us, and feeds us just enough.
when winter comes, where will we shelter,
what will we eat?
who are the ghosts that shadow and sing?
will they help or haunt?
heard and not seen,
do they intend or not to taunt?

do the others grannies hear them, too?
their silence piercing through
the children's din,
their songs mimicking the stream,
echoing the wind.
and now and then I see
a shadow that is not a tree,
a brightness that is not the moon
or sunlight in a glade.

sword woman wonders

my sword is free.
I keep it gleaming
through its waxing and its waning,
its rising and descent.

it knows no lover
but my hand, it pierces
nothing but the air.
who is there to defend?

softly, gently, we climb the mountain,
then descend. there are fish
gleaming in the river.
there are wild grapes within our reach.

there are voices I have never heard before,
muttered prayers, beseeching someone,
who? shall I answer? shall I part the veil?
my sword knows how, my sword.

look! a pig flies towards me
steed or meat?
the ground decides. I spring
and land between the wings.

raven talk

what is hard for the ones who only walk
is easy for us. easy
to perch on the highest rock
or the top of a dead tree,
easy to float on the wind
upside down, easy
to dive to the heart of a swamp.
our beaks are curved and golden,
our tails the envy of crows.
but our voices, oh, our voices
part the way between worlds,
veils, mists, stones, life, death.

you walkers can't fly but you can
follow our cry, if you dare,
if you dare.

bear grumbles

I don't mind sharing the berries,
there are enough,
or even the fish they manage to catch.
I hope they will leave
the bee trees alone,
and grubs of all kinds.

will they want more?
will they disturb my peace?
they no longer pay their way
with garbage.

I thought their kind was all gone.
who are these wrinkled ones
with their noisy cubs?

where will they go
when it's cold?

Ruby dreams of her garden

first there are beetles in the roses,
turning the leaves to rusty lace,
eating the morning bloom before noon.

(what is it like to eat a new-opened rose?
to consume heaven?
to devour the dawn of the world?)

then the beetles blow away
on a salt wind come all the way
from sea to mountain.

my roses bloom.
I am a rose, my petals
will last for a day.
my sweetness has a power
far beyond form.
bees know the truth
of my heart.

sorrow singer calls for courage singer

where are you old comrade, old foe
with your songs of exhortation?
we have lifted our voices together
in harmonic dissonance,
clashing, comforting, now and then
resolving the teeth-jangling half notes
to one pure sound. oh, how it hurts

to remember sweetness, life
before and after loss. how do
these wizened old women carry on,
feeding and naming and loving
the young when all has been
lost, and may yet again be
lost? shall I join them? how? when

I am nothing more than an endless song?
loo loo loooo aiyee way lo, looooo....
in this land of stone my voice goes
on and on, in this land of roaring water
my voice is lost in the falling of falls.
grandmothers, grandmothers,
I am older and more weary than you all.

I will call on courage singer
to sing for you, but wait! I will sing, too,
wrap you around and rock you
in song. you who cradle the children
need to be cradled, too. I will be
your lullaby, so soft, you'll hardly hear...
loo loo aiyee way lo aiyee way looooo

courage singer answers

mine is morning song, blankets thrown back,
stiff limbs unfurled, cold or bracing dew,
heavy cloud or sun piercing through.
the birds sing, and I will sing, too. I know
my old friend, from you, the courage it takes
to let sleep go, to know you have to face
it all again, when you would rather
let go, once and for all, at last let go.
so I will sing courage, look! the banked coals
leap into flame, there is peas porridge in the pot.
hi, ho, for another day, for one more chance.
let's take it, it's all we've got.

storm singer explains

the mountains are my playmates,
we toss wind back and forth,
we clear or spear clouds.
I bring the mercy of lightning
when the air is heavy and green.
I do not mean harm,
grannies, children, I mean
change.

Abelia sings to herself

they called me after the flowers,
the flowers made the air so sweet,
sweet as her skin, when she had milk.
I wanted to eat the air, and I did.
doesn't your breath go inside you?
I'd stand under the bush,
close my eyes, and breathe.
for days and days it's all I did,
and I wasn't ever hungry at all.
and then the flowers turned brown
and fell and lay in the dirt.
then...they disappeared.
where did they go, where does
everything go? where did my mama go?
where will I go when I disappear?

the flying pig ponders

she called me into being,
although maybe I *was* already,
something live searching,
rooting among roots.
she called me into being,
something that could fly.
soon I will breathe fire.
it's better than being bacon,
better to fry than to be fried.
ha! better to fly than to be hog-tied.

Ruby crosses the stream

the stream flows the way it always flows
down down down away down,
curling back on itself
in foaming waves, in heaving, weaving,
backward waves.

slowly, slowly each step an age,
I cross, finding places to lodge
this foot then that. I am a fleshy
stone, a tree fallen but still alive,
boughs leafing from brokenness.
I change the stream's song
with my wavering stand.

why not stand here forever?
what is on the other side? ah, a rock,
moss and mud almost dry after flood,
a place in the sun to sit and watch
the water round the bend,
coming and going, coming and going.
I lower my sit bones onto the rock.
the water slows around my feet.

where I've just walked
the water churns and foams and sings,
swift or slow, swift or slow,
high or low, here or there.
everywhere the water flows
is where it is.

the grannies in the storm

we've found shelter
among the rocks' haphazard roofs
that sluice the water away from us.
here we'll bide with some creature's bones,
older than ours, some snake's shed skin,
left behind as we would ours, if we could.
we'll grind it into a powder,
yes, and make it a tea, a snake slough tea.

the children are restless.
they don't want to huddle here.
we can't stop them, so we say,
all right, all right!
go out in the rain!
but first take off your rags,
leave them behind in the dry.
now, go run naked in the rain,
the warm mother rain.
that's right, little birds,
tilt back your heads,
open your mouths,
drink the sky.

temple sweeper gathers the seeds

I never mind the rain,
the touch of the gods.
but seeds on the stone
what if they wash away?
will they grow or be gone?
here is an empty jar
that once held wine.

(he drank it all, the one
I've brought here. on his tongue
rain turns to wine)

he says, we'll gather the seeds one by one,
the two of us together.
we'll take them to the ones
who hunger, the ones who
will know what they're for.

grey mouse

I watch hidden in the thick tangles of briars.
I am hungry, but if the seeds grow,
there will be more,

if I live. I am an old mouse now,
a lonely elephant without a herd.
grey, grey, rain, ghosts.
the grey cat still watches,
from where I don't know.

a blackberry beckons me.
I nibble gently,
ah, sweet dark rain.

the scribe catches the scent

they have brought that story with them,
that old, old story of hunger,
of searching for food,
of wanting to stay alive
for no other reason than to be alive.
how will it end this time?
will it ever end?

the man who does not speak creeps closer

I know what they have fled,
I know what has been done to them,
what I did once,
what I have done.

there is a sound hidden,
hiding in the hollow
under my chest.

if I let it out, the mountain might fall,
the children be crushed
under stone.

but if I don't speak,
I can never
atone.

morose fool shares

I will follow him now,
the silent man.
the boy and the goat have found a home.
the man who does not speak
knows my failure,
I know his.

I have found hazelnuts.
I will crack them open with my hard head.
I will share them with him.

we will make our words and silence
wise.

Lapis Lazuli's lullaby

loo loo aiyee way lo aiyee way looooo....
sleep, my children, sleep,
sleep, my sister grannies, too.
loo loo aiyee way lo aiyee way looooo....
the high wind makes moan with me,
the soft wind, from a far place, sweet and salt,
the harsh wind, bitter with the memory of smoke,
the wind close as breath, distant as home.
loo loo aiyee way lo aiyee way looooo....
sleep, my children, sleep,
heavy heads on bony breast and knee,
young warmth keeping me warm.
sleep, my weary sisters, sleep.
we have traveled so hard, climbing rock stairs
to the place of rivers and stars.
who knows where we are,
who knows where we really are.
loo loo aiyee way lo aiyee way looooo....
maybe it's enough that we've come this far
to a place where the end begins again.
loo loo aiyee way lo aiyee way looooo....

Goat Boy in the night

the others are asleep,
curled in little heaps.
it is warm with them and soft,
except for the elbows and knees.

I followed him here, the man
with the cap that lost its bells,
and my mother followed me.
she is *my* mother still,

though she lets the grannies take
her milk to feed all the children.
she is tired, can't they see?
tired from making so much milk

for so many more than me.
I like to play with the others,
but I miss the time before
they were here. while they snore

I creep out of the cave onto the crag.
they don't know how to climb.
my mother taught me. I scramble
to her now, where she stands

between the cliff and the milky
spill of stars. the pig is there, too.
she did not climb, she flew with wings
we can't always see. she snorts

small sparks that leap
and fall to the darkest dark.
my mother doesn't tell me to go back.
the pig doesn't tell me what to do.

they know I know what
the others can't, and so
we stand close together and watch
and with our friend the night.

sword woman stands watch

I stand too, sword at the ready,
blade slim as the waning moon,
supple as living sinew,
quieter than those unquiet bones.

can't they hear her following them?
the woman with the floating skirt,
the man weaving after her? can't they hear
the skeleton rattling a plea to them, or warning?

I can see those two outlined in stars,
she with a jar on her head,
he clutching one to his chest.
now and then, he lifts it to his lips,

then sputtering lowers it. seeds, seeds,
no drink, no drink. his sigh turns to song,
hey ho, hey ho from temple high
to cave below my love and I will go, will go.

the grey cat sees

most will think it just a rock
jutting against the sky.
I am the grey cat, I slip
from one world to another
as easily as breath
in and out, in and out.
I know when to wait,
I know when to pounce.
I am waiting for you,
little friend, little mouse.
lift your long trunk to the stars.
with your wide grey ears
make a great wind.
your tiny dream may yet grow big,
and soon you will dream with me.

courage singer waits

dawn is searching out their cave,
touching the curve of the jars
left for them in the night.
even the most wakeful still sleep.
it takes courage to open your eyes,
courage to plant seeds,
courage to hope they will grow.

I am here in the tiniest cracks.
I am the trickle of water
that greens the rocks' seams.
I am the hidden spring,
just waiting for someone
to scratch the dirt
and drink.

the silence of the stones

we will have the last word,
we will have the last silence.
even if the earth quakes,
even if the water
wears us away
and away.
still we have seen it all.
we bear witness
to all folly and bravery,
to all struggle, all defeat.
but we won't speak those words.
we don't judge,
we render silence.
beautiful bones, one day you will all be
beautiful bones,
like us.

ancient dreamer dreams on

the mountain thinks it's old,
but I am older.
I am stars and dust and ocean.
I am the lap
that will hold you all
in the end, beyond the end.
oh, my children, my wilted flowers,
my fallen trees and heroes,
my scrabbling, swimming creatures,
my crying, flying winged ones,
come home, come home
all is lost and never lost.
come home to me,
come home.

www.ingramcontent.com/pod-product-compliance
Lightning Source LLC
Chambersburg PA
CBHW022038090426
42741CB00007B/1113